Animal Fun Facts

FUN FACTS ABOUT SHARKS

by Julie Murray

Dash!
LEVELED READERS
An Imprint of Abdo Zoom • abdobooks.com

2

Dash!
LEVELED READERS

Level 1 – Beginning
Short and simple sentences with familiar words or patterns for children who are beginning to understand how letters and sounds go together.

Level 2 – Emerging
Longer words and sentences with more complex language patterns for readers who are practicing common words and letter sounds.

Level 3 – Transitional
More developed language and vocabulary for readers who are becoming more independent.

THIS BOOK CONTAINS RECYCLED MATERIALS

abdobooks.com

Published by Abdo Zoom, a division of ABDO, PO Box 398166, Minneapolis, Minnesota 55439.

Printed in the United States of America, North Mankato, Minnesota.
052021
092021

Photo Credits: Alamy, BluePlanetArchive.com, iStock, Shutterstock
Production Contributors: Kenny Abdo, Jennie Forsberg, Grace Hansen, John Hansen
Design Contributors: Candice Keimig, Neil Klinepier

Library of Congress Control Number: 2020919495

Publisher's Cataloging in Publication Data

Names: Murray, Julie, author.
Title: Fun facts about sharks / by Julie Murray
Description: Minneapolis, Minnesota : Abdo Zoom, 2022 | Series: Animal fun facts | Includes online resources and index.
Identifiers: ISBN 9781098224486 (lib. bdg.) | ISBN 9781098225421 (ebook) | ISBN 9781098225896 (Read-to-Me ebook)
Subjects: LCSH: Sharks--Juvenile literature. | Sharks--Behavior--Juvenile literature. | Marine fishes—Behavior--Juvenile literature. | Questions and answers--Juvenile literature. | Animal behavior--Juvenile literature.
Classification: DDC 597.3--dc23

Table of Contents

Fun Facts About Sharks

Sharks live throughout the world's ocean. There are more than 500 shark **species**.

Sharks have been swimming around for 450 million years. That is 220 million years before the dinosaurs!

Bull sharks can live in both salt and freshwater. They have been found in the Mississippi River!

Most sharks have 5 to 15 rows of teeth. They lose teeth almost every day. New ones grow. Some sharks lose 35,000 teeth during their lifetime!

Sharks have **placoid scales**. These make a shark's skin feel like sandpaper. The scales point toward the tail. This helps sharks move easily through water.

The mako shark is the fastest shark. It can swim up to 80 miles per hour (129 km/h). Its body is shaped like a torpedo. It is made for speed!

The great white shark has a strong sense of smell. It can smell a small amount of blood up to 3 miles (5 km) away!

The dwarf lantern shark is the smallest shark **species**. It is less than 7 inches (18 cm) long.

That is small enough to fit in the palm of your hand!

The whale shark is a type of **carpet shark**. It is the largest shark **species**.

It is also the biggest fish in the world! It can grow up to 40 feet (12 m) long. It can weigh up to 47,000 pounds (22,320 kg)!

Animal Spotlight

Great Hammerhead Shark

Size: Up to 20 feet (6.1 m) long; Up to 1,000 pounds (453.5 kg)

Appearance: largest hammerhead species with dark gray body, lighter belly, hammer-shaped head

Range: warm and tropical seas worldwide

Habitat: often found in shallow waters near islands and reefs, and in lagoons

Diet: stingrays, other rays, bony fish

Lifespan: 20 to 30 years

Glossary

carpet shark – any of about 40 species of sharks that have blotched or spotted patterns on the body. Many species have barbels, are bottom-feeders, and are large in size.

placoid scales – also called denticles, spiny, tooth-like projections seen only in certain fish.

species – a group of living things that look alike, share a common name, and can have young with one another.

Index

Online Resources

Booklinks
NONFICTION NETWORK
FREE! ONLINE NONFICTION RESOURCES

To learn more about sharks, please visit **abdobooklinks.com** or scan this QR code. These links are routinely monitored and updated to provide the most current information available.